THE HIGH SCHOOL ATHLETE'S GAME PLAN

SCORING A COLLEGE ATHLETIC SCHOLARSHIP

A Sophomore, Junior and Senior Year
Guide for Players and Parents

BY ED SEIDICK

Copyright © 2019 Edward Charles Seidick

All rights reserved. This book or any portion thereof may not be reproduced or used in any manner whatsoever without the express written permission of the publisher except for the use of brief quotations in a book review.

Printed in the United States of America

First Printing, 2019

Revised 2022

TABLE OF CONTENTS

CHAPTER 1	Academic Actions to be Taken Prior to Junior Year	1
CHAPTER 2	Athletic Actions to be Taken Prior to Junior Year	6
CHAPTER 3	Academic Actions to be Taken During Junior Year	12
CHAPTER 4	Athletic Actions to be Taken During Junior Year	18
CHAPTER 5	Academic Actions to be Taken During Senior Year	24
CHAPTER 6	Athletic Actions to be Taken During Senior Year	30
CHAPTER 7	Key Areas of Consideration	35
CHAPTER 8	Contacting the Coach	38
CHAPTER 9	Campus Visit	42
CHAPTER 10	Admission Process	49
ADDENDUM	Pandemic Update	52
NOTES		56

Introduction

The intention of this guide is to share my many years of experience with you so that you can help your son or daughter reach their goals. Sadly, there are way too many parents who think their children are going to earn college athletic scholarships who simply don't understand the process. They tend to think that these things happen all at once or during their senior year. In reality, the athletic scholarship process begins well before that. Planning should begin much earlier.

First of all, you should be very happy that your son or daughter is talented enough to be even considering playing their sport in college. That said, you need to fully understand the process to take full advantage of all that is out there. While your child may not get that full ride to the top school and then go pro, the realistic goal is get the most money to offset the ever-rising cost of a quality college education. Many schools will offer grants in lieu of scholarships, but they are the same thing, a reduction in the cost of a college education due to athletic ability.

At the time of my writing this handbook, subsidized Federal Stafford loans are running at around 6.8% and bank loans are much more costly. These loans are basically tattooed on you as you can't escape them. You can't get away from them even if you declare bankruptcy. Most loans also require the parent to co-sign which makes the parents equally responsible for the repayment of the loan. The basic math says that if you borrow $40,000 to get your degree and take ten years to pay it back, you will have to pay $460 per month and pay over $15,000 in interest. These insane numbers are exactly why every dollar in scholarship or grant is worth the effort to get it. It does not matter what the school calls the money they give you, it just matters that they give it to you.

The National Collegiate Athletic Association (NCAA), The National Association of Intercollegiate Athletics (NAIA), and The National Junior College Athletic Association (NJCAA) programs are able to offer money to your son or daughter in many different ways. Since scholarships are limited, college coaches are also able to find grants and other ways to assist in paying for their program. The full ride options are not as plentiful as many think. Most schools want to spread the money around as much as they can to help fill their programs. Personally, I don't care what they call it as long as they are giving it.

I have been very fortunate to have gone through the recruitment process myself and to have coached dozens more that have been able to play at the college level and even a few that played professionally. There are a lot of tricks and strategies that I have been able to develop over a 30+ year coaching career. Some of them are obvious and others are much more under the radar. The purpose of this guide is to pass this on to you so that others are able to benefit from the things I have learned. As an economics teacher at the high school level, I am also frustrated by the costs of college and the manner in which banks and other loan agencies mistreat our children. It is fundamentally unfair to burden kids with the costs of the loans and to burden parents with the fear of failing their children. We need to find ways to mitigate those costs.

If you are reading this, you already know the sacrifice that your son or daughter has made to gain the skill set required to play at the college level. You, the parents, have also sacrificed. You have spent countless weekends running to games and missing meals to get to practices. You have already spent thousands on equipment and travel teams. Now it is time to get the reward. Over the length of this guide, I will give you the big picture on how to get as much money as you can to send your children to college. I will also offer subtle points that will aid you in talking to college coaches and how to pick the school that best suits your children.

Remember, about 7% of high school varsity athletes play in college and less than 2% of college athletes will go pro. The only sport where the number is above that is baseball, where it approaches 9%. But that is counting minor leagues where most do not earn a living wage. While many parents and athletes think they have the ability to go pro, most will not get there. The love your children have for the sports they play is already a great reward. But using that ability to get the best education possible is what this is really about. Chances are that if your son or daughter is talented enough to go pro, then this guide is not really for you. Those players will have college coaches fighting over them and smoothing out any issues that arise. This guide is for the kids who need scholarship/grant money in order to go college in the first place. This is for the parents who can't afford the best programs or the school that will most benefit their children.

Hopefully, you will pick up enough here to lead your children into the program that is best suited to set them up for the rest of their lives. It is going to take a lot of work, but it is well worth it. So, take it all in and then get started saving some money and putting your student-athlete on the road to success.

Chapter 1

Academic Actions to be Taken Prior to Junior Year

Hopefully you already know that you need to start planning for college athletics and academics long before the colleges start looking at your children. There are a lot of actions that you can take to set up your student-athlete early to make their lives easier. Each level of college play has specific academic requirements to be aware of as your children plan their high school schedules.

o **Meet with your Guidance Counselor about your high school academic plan**

The high school guidance counselors are usually experts in building the academic career necessary to participate in college sports. Many schools, including where I teach, have altered programming to fit these requirements. Any quality guidance counselor is up to date on the ever-changing rules. If you don't feel comfortable with the counselor your child is assigned, request a meeting with the principal to discuss your needs.

If you are starting the process after the freshman year, you may need to take summer courses or load up your schedule to meet your needs. Make sure the level and names of the courses meet the requirements of the level you hope your son or daughter will attend.

o **Review NCAA, NAIA, and NJCAA Academic Eligibility Requirements**

Trust the counselor, but verify what they tell you and your child. Each level has specific course names and levels that must be taken and these can change without much warning. They also may require a certain score in those classes. It is very important to start on track and stay there. These requirements can be found here:
NCAA eligibility (http://www.ncaa.org/student-athletes/play-division-i-sports)
NAIA eligibility (https://play.mynaia.org/)
NJCAA eligibility (http://njcaa.org/eligibility/index)

o   **Take challenging high school courses; advanced placement and honors courses are preferable for most colleges**

Colleges do not want to see student-athletes take courses that don't challenge them. Many of the colleges that your son or daughter will be considering are at the NCAA division III level and these schools are very focused on the academic piece. They may not be able to offer the scholarship, but they do offer grants/aid to get athletes into their schools so plan accordingly.

o   **Take the PSAT test and begin to examine SAT and ACT test books**

During your sophomore year, your son or daughter should take the PSAT and start to get a feel for what these tests are all about. Many schools are going away from these tests as an all-powerful score, but they are still important. If they can get a taste for these exams early, they can likely begin to improve their scores when the tests actually matter. There are plenty of study books and guides that are available at your school library or guidance office.

o   **Calculate your Grade Point Average and find out your class rank**

This will become repetitive, but you should be mindful of where your son or daughter stands academically. Grade Point Average and class rank are not as impactful with college admission offices as they once were, but they do still matter. Colleges do understand that the GPA may be lower than desired if academically challenging classes show up on the transcript. Most high schools are already aware of this and weight classes accordingly. Keep up to date on these numbers so that your son or daughter can keep improving them.

o   **Speak to your Guidance Counselor about the college search resources available to guide your decision**

Thankfully, the internet has made this process much easier, but the vast majority of college and aptitude searches require payment. Most high schools have accounts with several of these search resources and your counselors will help walk your son or daughter through the process. Believe it or not, these college search/professional suggestion sites are far more accurate than those most of us took them in school 30 years ago. They are much more likely to find out what your children are genuinely interested in and offer potential career options. They also can match you up with college programs.

o **Develop positive relationships with your teachers**

Ok, this sounds simple, but it is more important than most think. These teachers will be writing letters of recommendation, talking to other teachers that your children will have in future years, and they will offer support and advice along the way. You never know who will be able to help you with a contact or some timely advice. In one school year alone, I typically write over 30 recommendation letters. The better I know the student, the better the letter will be. Teachers can also assist with college applications and the essay that goes with it.

o **Develop good study habits as time management and writing skills are very important at the college level**

If your son or daughter wants to play a sport at the collegiate level, they will have to budget their time wisely. Many times, the more intelligent and talented students do not need to study or work very hard at the high school level. This will change in college. Many athletes already understand the commitment to their craft, but since most will not go pro, the studies need to stay strong. The earlier they develop these skills, the easier it will be later when free time becomes more scarce. Colleges also want to see students that are well-rounded and do more than just play sports. They want students that are active in their school and their community. They want student-athletes who prove they can handle the workload that will come with playing college sports.

As far as writing goes, hopefully your local school district spends enough time on creative writing and doesn't just focus on responses for standardized testing. The ability to think and write quickly will become very important at the college level as time constraints increase. Colleges also require an entry essay that will play a role in acceptance.

o **Focus on a wide variety of subjects at school to expose yourself to many possible majors**

You never know what subject or which teachers will turn a kid onto a career. I doubt most of my freshman or sophomore teachers would have ever expected me to become a teacher, but one of my junior year teachers turned me onto history in a way I never expected could happen. If I hadn't had that class with that teacher, I am not sure where I would be at this point. The more exposure to a variety subjects, the better the odds of finding a possible major. Schools will certainly accept "undecided" students, but a solid idea of a major is a better way to match the student-athlete with the best college program.

o **Consider involvement in various extracurricular activities (clubs, mentoring, etc.) as well-rounded students are given more consideration at the college level**

Again, the more active your son or daughter is in their school community, the more a college will be willing to offer them grants and scholarships. Colleges are moving more in this direction every year. School involvement has surpassed ACT or SAT scores for many colleges. They want students who can juggle a full schedule and remain highly skilled athletes. They also will note what year(s) they were involved in clubs and activities. If they only see involvement during their senior year, that will be a red flag. Your school will likely offer a wide-range of clubs that will require different levels of commitment. Find those that fit your schedule and plans.

o **Create a filing system for any college information you receive or collect**

Although colleges are not allowed to have direct contact with athletes at this point, that doesn't stop you from collecting information. Many high school and travel coaches have contacts at local colleges or at schools that have recruited in your school before. I suggest using a tiered system for each level. You need to divide up NCAA, NAIA, and NJCAA information as they are very different. You also should divide up local schools and those that are further away. I also suggest having a "dream school" folder. Along the way, you can add or subtract information and options. It would also be wise to create a possible majors folder to gather information that can be cross-matched later. You can also create lists that can be added to along the way.

o **Begin to think of your career goals and areas of academic interest**

Most kids are not ready to begin thinking about a career at this age, but it is always easier to work backwards when looking at potential careers. Your children likely have subjects that they excel in, so start there and start exploring some options in those subjects. This doesn't need to be written in stone, but the earlier your start, the easier it will be later.

o **Volunteer within the school or your community**

The coach of your college of choice may have to sell your son or daughter to an admissions office. Volunteer work goes a long way toward impressing admissions offices. As stated earlier, they are beginning to value the whole student-athlete and not just the SAT or ACT score. They would rather admit the kid who is ranked 100-150 in their class who volunteers with at-need students, at the local food bank, or at their church instead of the kid who is ranked 20th and doesn't do anything besides play a sport. This is also a very important part of getting grants or scholarships that are available.

o **Explore what area of the country where you may wish to attend college**

This is hard as most younger student-athletes fantasize about moving far from home, but realistically, the sport they play may also impact this decision. If they play baseball, softball, golf, or any other sport that is weather dependent, that may push them toward warmer areas. Start to think about where family or family friends may be living and what options that may help with. Consider taking a family vacation or at least spending time looking at the type of environment your son or daughter may want to live in. Also make sure to understand that most small schools prefer area athletes over those coming from further away as it is easier to scout and develop relationships that way.

Chapter 2

Athletic Actions to be Taken Prior to Junior Year

Assuming your son or daughter has the skill necessary to be looking to play at the collegiate level, there is a lot to be done prior to the usual recruitment period. Some of this is obvious, but necessary to state. However, having gone through this many times, there are a lot of things that parents do not realize they need to do or when to do them.

o **Realistically assess your athletic abilities**

Please don't be "that parent". When looking at your children's athletic ability, don't overvalue it. Don't sell them on some big career that has them shunning their studies because they begin to believe your hype or the hype of coaches who don't know what they are talking about. Travel and AAU coaches may tell you how great your kids are and how much potential they have. Sadly, some coaches are in it just for the money and they will say anything to keep that income flowing. Keep in mind that anyone you pay has financial motives when offering their assessment. Be careful not to fall victim to false praise meant only to keep you paying for the privilege of playing on a particular team.

Too many also think that the large Division I schools will come calling and don't prepare for reality. While, reality might be that your son or daughter is good enough to get grants to play at the Division III level and get a great education rather than getting into their / your dream school. Please take the time to get real input about their chances. Don't yell at high school coaches who don't have the same view of your son or daughter's talent, get an explanation on why that view is different. It might be a small thing, but players need that honest view if they want to play at the next level. Start early so they can be ready. However, you also have to be careful to not dampen their dream as a lot can change in a few years.

So much can be written here about understanding the true potential of your child. I have watched parents become so pushy that all of the local schools refused to even look at an athlete that usually would fit their needs. The parents honest and realistic approach is important. Parents get a reputation that spreads just as fast, if not faster, than that of their child. Also understand that there have been so many athletes that were berated and driven so hard that they no longer wanted to play. It is good to support them, but don't push them. In addition, please have them play multiple sports! Specialization in one sport is not helpful. If your child only wants to play one sport, then please take time off. At least 2 months of rest is imperative to maintaining a healthy body. It is not healthy mentally, nor physically, to only participate in one sport. The muscles become overused and injuries become far more likely.

o **Talk to all of your coaches about college athletics**

Again, all of coaches that your player interacts with will have a different view on their skill set. All it takes is that one coach who believes in them and can sell them to a college. Many of the coaches at the high school level played in college. Seek real guidance from them and their honest evaluations. However, don't be discouraged if you son or daughter isn't starting on the varsity team as a freshman, there is still a lot of time for physical growth and development. As long as your player has the dream to play at college, keep fanning that flame as you never know where hard work will take them. Even if they don't end up getting that Division I scholarship, maybe they can still use athletics to play at a smaller school and cut thousands of dollars off your tuition bills. That is the ultimate goal here, right? Plus, that work ethic and determination will help them for the rest of their lives.

o **Become familiar with the NCAA, NAIA, and NJCAA rules and regulations governing athletic recruitment**

This is a vital piece! You must know when they can contact you and your kids and how they can make that contact. There are different restrictions at each level and you must be careful to know them. I can't imagine most parents want their children playing for a coach who is already violating the rules before their son or daughter is even in that program. Coaches like this are not likely to stick at these schools and your son or daughter will have to deal with a coaching change and, as we will discuss later, that is certainly not an ideal situation.

These rules can change without much notice, so keep up to date on them. Although the coaches are not allowed to talk to you or your child until a certain age/date, that doesn't mean they can't observe them from afar. The bigger the college, the more help the head coaches have in the recruitment process. These coaches/recruiters don't always advertise themselves so it is always wise to put your best foot forward at all times. For exact information on these rules, please visit the individual websites for each level of play. Again, these rules change year-by-year and also have differing restraints and timelines for particular sports.

o **Learn about the different levels of competition within the college setting (NCAA Division I, II, III, NAIA, and Junior Colleges)**

This one is self-explanatory, but many people have misconceptions about these various levels. Each level has their own attractions and potential downfalls. While playing NCAA Division I is more likely to get you into a professional career, I can't tell you how often I have seen players head to the wrong school with the wrong coach just to say they went D-I. Kids that play at smaller schools often get more playing time and enjoy college much more than those that go to the wrong school just to make that D-I claim. Big fish, small pond - or - little fish, big pond. That is a tough choice, but one that should be made carefully and knowing what each level offers is very important.

Visiting local colleges and attending games early in the process can be very helpful. Seeing the environment and atmosphere of the school and team can be enlightening. Some small schools offer a more competitive and fun experience than some Division I schools. Get the feel for these things as early as possible.

o **Create a file of your achievements: newspaper clippings, TV highlights, internet articles, awards received, etc.)**

With social media and local news coverage, student-athletes are getting more press than ever. Keep an organized inventory of each time your son or daughter's name is mentioned in the press. Take screenshots of team web-sites that offer statistics. Record TV coverage and make a highlight reel and video file. If your team records each game and has a website that you have access to, record as much as you can and spend the time to edit highlights as well. Know that college coaches don't like highlight video as they doesn't show the full player. They want to see games with their own eyes or at least watch whole games on tape. But that highlight video may get the college coach in the gym or on the field to watch.

o **Develop athletic goals for each year of high school**

These should be realistic, but not so easy that they are attained without much work. Making varsity as a sophomore or gaining that starting spot are examples of goals that players should have at this point. However, they also need to start looking at team goals. The better the team, the more college coaches will see them. You never know who is watching other players on your team or even on other teams so the goal of always getting better is usually a good place to start. One of my high school teammates got a scholarship from a school that came to see me play. This happens more often than you might think.

o **Send an initial contact letter to college coaches**

Although they can't contact you yet, contacting college coaches at schools in your area and those you may be interested in is a good place to start before the recruitment process fully begins. Getting your son or daughter's name out there never hurts. These coaches spend a lot of time recruiting and while they may come to a game to look at another player, they will remember your contact letter and look for your son or daughter at the same time. These coaches keep very organized files for recruitment and do not like to lose out on local athletes.

This letter should contain academic areas of interest, camps attended, high school schedule, travel team schedules, and general information about why you are interested in their school. Make sure to let your high school coaches know what schools you have contacted so they are prepared to talk with those coaches. You never want your coach to be caught off guard. Sometimes, college coaches will seek out the high school coach right after a game and you want them to be ready for these conversations. This is where those solid relationships with coaches come in handy.

o **Fill out questionnaires from any colleges you may be interested in**

Each college has online questionnaires that can be filled out before the junior year. Take advantage of this and get on their mailing list as early as you can. Some college admission offices look at such things and if you are interested in them early, it is to your advantage when it comes down to their decision making time.

o **Attend camps, clinics, and pro try-out days during the summer to become familiar with your competition and expose your skills to college coaches**

It is in your benefit to know the competition. Schools only have so much money to offer to athletes and they will not double up on certain positions. For example, if a team has a junior starting at your position, they will be less likely to want you as an incoming freshman as they will already have a freshman at that spot. If they have a senior starting, they likely have a sophomore as well and will be looking for someone else at that spot for the next year. They prefer to balance a senior-sophomore and a junior-freshman at each position.

Find the camps and clinics the coaches of your target schools are working in the summer or over winter break. Head to those if possible and make sure to have your son or daughter introduce themselves. They can't talk about their sport, but they can quickly say hello and your strong first impression will be remembered. It is also helpful to attend these camps as you may impress a coach who doesn't need you, but he might know someone who can. Also, getting a better idea of your competition can't hurt as it will let you know where you stand and let you know what level of college to begin looking at. Many local college coaches also have other jobs and need to supplement their income by doing these camps. They also want to get an early look at possible recruits. These camps can be the start of a great relationship!

o **Familiarize yourself with the coaches of colleges you may be interested in attending**

No one wants to go to a college only for the coach to abandon ship after one year. You need to begin familiarizing yourselves with the coaches and their styles. Some players like to play for a fiery coach and others like the softer touch. Know what you are looking for. This is also helpful in knowing what the coaches look like so you know when they are in attendance. Become as familiar as possible with their style and system as you can so that you can have the early feel for what you would be getting. The coach-player relationship is vital for success. It also impacts the academic side of things so be sure to know what you are getting. The best way to do that is to start early.

o **Take unofficial visits to return questionnaires and get a feel for the college**

If you and your children have the time and the means, then an unofficial visit to some colleges of choice is a great idea. If you have filled out those questionnaires, print them out and take them to the school to hand deliver them. These are the things that can differentiate you from the competition and can also help you get a vibe about the schools. Remember, it is a two-way street. You have to make your son or daughter desirable to the school, but they also need to be desirable to you. If the school is local, attend as many games as you can.

o **Parents should introduce themselves to college coaches that attend your games, even if they didn't come to see just you.**

A quick handshake and conversation will get your child's name on their mind. Start this relationship as soon as possible. You can also get a feel for the type of person these coaches are. You are trying to get them to have a favorable impression of your son or daughter, but you also need to get a favorable impression of them. Do they talk to you or blow you off? Do they give you a positive impression? This initial meeting gives you the opportunity to make a positive or negative impression.

o **Be aware that you are evaluated by coaches that don't advertise themselves as well – so always do your best**

Many college coaches love to wear their school colors and logos wherever they go. Others try to be very subtle. Those that are not seeking attention are at the games to see what your sons and daughters are doing when they don't know they are being watched. These coaches are looking at one or two specific players and always hopeful to be surprised by a kid they didn't already know about. Hopefully as a younger player, your son or daughter can offer that surprise.

o **Video tape your games for potential use later in preparing a highlight video**

Many high schools are now taping games and using that video online for study and evaluation. If they offer you access to that, use it and download what you can. If it lets you make a highlight tape, do that as well. If your school is not able to tape all games, get yourself a quality video camera and learn how to use it. Tape as many games as you can for different angles that you can have ready for potential coaches.

Chapter 3

Academic Actions to be Taken During Junior Year

Now that you have made it this far, you need to understand the importance of the junior year. It is often the most important year of high school as far as colleges are concerned. They want to see growth and maturity. The following academic tips are among the most important things colleges will look at and among those that can make the difference between getting a scholarship or not. I don't think the value of this year can be overstated when talking about scholarships/grants. Your son or daughter must make academics a strong priority during the junior year. If they have struggled in 9th and 10th grade, the growth and improvement will show the prospective schools that maturity has occurred. If they have been solid all along, then continued success in the classroom will be very impactful to prospective schools.

o **Review college search resources with your Guidance Counselor**

Please keep taking advantage of as many resources as you can. Guidance counselors are the best such resource that your child will have to use at their school. If your child is assigned a good one, they will be a great sounding board and help you in many ways. Make sure that you are all comfortable with this relationship as these counselors are very important in this process. There are a lot of college search options that schools have access to that you do not. They will be able to provide insight into specific programs and what is required for those programs. They can give you and your son or daughter a better overall view of each school and keep you headed in the proper direction. Also know that many high schools have cooperative enrollment programs with local Junior and Community Colleges. As the year progresses, explore these options to start earning college credits.

o **Explore College Guides in guidance office, at the library, or online**

Again, your guidance office will likely have resources that are not as easily available to you at home. This is especially true for the local colleges and universities. The counselors may also have some contacts within some local schools and inside certain programs that you can use to your advantage. This is another reminder to find a good counselor! These guides can be found at school, but you can also access them at your local library and find them in your local bookstores. Be sure to use the current issue as some of the rules change from year to year.

o **Review NCAA and NAIA Academic Eligibility Requirements and evaluate your academic progress**

These requirements can change and do so without much warning. Keep up to date on this as the responsibility ultimately falls on the family, not on the schools. You should also make an appointment with the guidance counselors to make sure that your son or daughter is taking all of the correct courses and is meeting all necessary requirements. It will be too late to make major adjustments during the senior year, but you can still do this during the junior year. Trust the counselors, but also make sure to verify what they tell you. In the end, their mistake will hurt your son or daughter, so be careful.

o **Continue to take challenging courses, advanced placement or honors**

The junior year is a great indicator of the type of student the colleges will be getting. Take more difficult courses when possible and keep improving your grades. Reaching at least the lowest honors level will be useful when applying to schools. If your school offers more GPA credit for harder courses, keep that in mind when filling out the schedule. If they don't, your son or daughter may have a lower class rank and knowing why is important with college admissions offices. Many high schools are moving away from class rank, but that does not mean the colleges will ignore the type of courses taken.

o **Take SAT or ACT test multiple times and have scores sent to the top schools on your list**

Okay, as a high school teacher I know how ridiculous standardized testing has become and how our students are over-saturated with them. Your children have likely taken more standardized tests in the past year than you did in all of your years in school. Thankfully, colleges understand this and will look at your child as more than just a test score. That said however, they still have requirements and minimums that they will accept. Taking these tests multiple times is very important. You also need to look at which test your goal schools accept. After looking at the tests, understand what each one emphasizes and how your child's strengths may match up. There are many books out there to help your child study for these tests and to assist in the test taking skill. Evaluate them before buying them, but if your child is one who struggles to score well on standardized testing, they are worth the price.

o **Calculate and evaluate your GPA and class rank**

It is never a bad idea to know where your child stands and this will also help determine future plans. Knowing this information off the top of your head can also help when communicating with coaches and any scouts that may ask. If these numbers are not good enough, start planning now on how to improve them. If they are where you want to be, plan how to keep them there. Again, these numbers don't always tell the whole story as some school districts are more academically rigorous than others, but colleges and universities already know what schools are better than others. Being ranked 75th in a challenging district with a 500+ graduating class might be worth more than being ranked 25th in a small district with a less than stellar reputation. Keep this in mind!

o **Continue to develop positive relationships with your teachers**

The teachers that your son or daughter has during their junior year will be the most likely ones to write letters of recommendation. They will be the ones your children go to during the Fall of their senior year for these letters or when they start to apply for early acceptance. The better this relationship is, the more complimentary their recommendation will be. I have written dozens of these letters and can personally attest to this. Since I have started teaching an honors 11th grade class, the number of students asking for a letter from me has skyrocketed. The adjectives and superlatives I use are dependent upon the impression that student left with me. Most of my students perform well academically, but some make a more indelible mark on me.

o **Begin a list of possible teachers to write recommendation letters**

Your child may want to ask other seniors or older students about which teachers write the best letters. Some teachers are very short and to the point while others use more flattering language. Get this list started as teachers tend to be hit with these requests the most during the first 2 months of school and the last month of school. If you can figure this out earlier, you can make requests at times when your letter will be more individual and thoughtful. Those that ask at the end of their junior year give me more time to write a strong letter. Once the Fall arrives and a teacher is inundated with requests, some get lost in the shuffle.

o **Continue good study and time management habits**

These skills will continue to become more ingrained in your kids as time goes on. The junior year is incredibly busy for the normal junior looking to get into a good school. This is even more true when your son or daughter is trying to get money to play a sport in college. Trying to juggle sports, training, jobs, and academics can get very difficult at this point. Keeping a schedule and priorities will be helpful.

o **Attend college fairs**

Every Fall, most high schools will have a college fair of some type. You need to be there. Many communities also have college fairs at convention centers or other large buildings. Look for when these are and plan ahead. The contacts that you make at these events may have a strong influence on acceptance into their schools. A positive first impression may make that crucial difference. Most admissions offices send representatives to these fairs and they are great sources of correct information and can become strong advocates when the time is right.

o **Continue to be involved in extracurricular activities and clubs**

Remember that you are looking for money any way you can get it. If a school wants to give you grant money instead of a scholarship, this is one of the best ways to get that money. Schools love the well-rounded student-athlete and involvement with clubs and other activities will show your kid's determination to fit that bill. These clubs may also lead into a decision on which major they want to have in college.

o **Seek input from friends, teachers, coaches, and alumni on various college programs and potential fit**

Any source is a good source. Meaning, if you like and respect a person's opinion, use them and value their views. If you don't like someone or have a negative view of their opinion, that may also give you some useful information. You can never have enough input on your college choices. You may learn about the food, the campus structure and class sizes. You may get a feel for the atmosphere and social setting. You may gain an understanding of the faculty and the college's academic standards. Add any of this information into your folders as you don't want to get confused later. With the onslaught of information available online, you can likely also find many stories from alumni and graduates from the athletic program.

o **Begin to think about your vision of the ideal college setting**

This is a tough one as you may not have a great idea what you and your children are looking for until you have a lot of information or have had a chance to visit a particular school. But this is when you need to start narrowing down the setting of your ideal school. I have seen many student-athletes go off to city schools only to transfer quickly back to the more suburban school setting they had in high school. I have also seen kids think they want the small school only to get there and be bored by the student life and social settings. Think long and hard about this as you don't want to make a mistake. Your ideal school may not have your ideal setting. Both are important in making this decision so you don't have to revisit it in a year. Don't undervalue the social aspect of the school.

o **Talk to your children about your financial abilities and each of your expected contributions**

This is never an easy discussion. A small grant or scholarship to the $40,000 a year school will not cut the costs to match those of the state schools. Many times, the local community and junior colleges can offer a cheap two-year option and then your son or daughter can get that scholarship for just their last two years. You need to be honest about this so that expectations are clear and everyone understands what is needed. If you are only able to cover $5,000 per year, start calculating what the loan costs would be and what possible major your student is looking at. You don't want to carry $50,000 in loans for a career that only plays $30,000 per year. This will impact a lot, be honest with yourselves. For a general idea, you can always play around with college loan calculators that are available online.

o **Obtain information about local scholarships and what is available from your top college choices**

Many schools have award banquets and offer scholarship money that is distributed through the school. These awards are usually in honor of an alumni or past athlete looking to help someone. Find all of these that you can through your guidance counselor and even your youth sports associations. Make the necessary contact with the groups that disperse the money and ask about the requirements. Then make it a point to meet as many of those requirements as possible because every dollar counts and makes a difference in the end.

o **Apply for financial aid and scholarships**

Okay, this is the toughest and most complex part of your junior year academic needs. You and your son or daughter need to start the process for financial aid as early as possible. The amount of documentation required is mind-blowing and the sooner you start, the more likely you are to get some money. Even if you are anticipating a full-ride, you need to do this in case something happens to change your mind or an unfortunate injury is suffered. This is also vital because most scholarships are only partial and grants never cover the full amount owed. Federal student aid is available at www.fafsa.ed.gov and most states also have programs available.

o **Consider applying for Early Decision**

Many schools offer Early Decision for top students. If your child is in a strong academic position and is fairly confident in heading to a school, this is a smart tactic to start getting the money flowing. College coaches love to lock up players as early as possible and if you have been able to forge that type of relationship and interest, take advantage of it. But make sure to get things in writing from the coach so that they don't pull your money to offer to another player that is making a late decision. This is where the letters of intent come into play as will be discussed later.

Chapter 4

Athletic Actions to be Taken During Junior Year

This is going to be a very busy year. Perhaps the most important time period when looking to play a sport in college. Make sure to put yourself in the best situations and don't spread yourself too thin. Camps, clinics, and off-season teams are great, but if your body is worn down or not in condition, these can hurt more than help.

o **Register with the NCAA Clearinghouse**

If you want to earn and use a scholarship to play at the DI or DII level of the NCAA, you must register and be cleared by the NCAA itself. The Eligibility Center operates within the NCAA to determine academic eligibility and verifies the amateur status of your child. You will not be able to play at those levels without going through this process. This can be completed later, but to avoid the backlog and possible delays, you should start this as early as the Fall of your junior year. Visit https://web3.ncaa.org/ecwr3/ for more information and to begin the process.

o **Obtain a current copy of *NCAA Guide for the College-Bound Student Athlete* from the NCAA**

This is an amazing guide for athletic eligibility at the DI and DII levels of the NCAA and well worth the low cost. Hopefully, your school guidance office will already have a copy, but if they don't, you can purchase it online. It will help with initial issues and adjustments you may need to make. This is updated almost every year so make sure the copy you have is current.

o **Know the NCAA, NAIA, and NJCAA rules and regulations about athletic recruitment by July 1st before your senior year**

These are different for each level. You must know what is allowed and what is not allowed. There are different rules for parents and kids. Your high school coaches can talk to the college coaches at any time, but the athlete can't. Go on the NCAA, NAIA, and NJCAA official websites for the exact details, but be sure to keep them straight so you keep within the rules. This will help you know which college coaches have morals and which are willing to cut corners. The corner cutters are usually the ones that won't last your child's full 4 years in college. Forget the stuff you hear about the football and basketball powerhouse schools and their recruitment issues. Chances are probably very high that if you are reading this, your child is not one that has to worry about alumni coming in with cars and cash to influence your decisions. Much more likely is that your child is looking to cut college costs and continue playing the sport they love. Most coaches will follow the rules, but some won't. Which type do you want around your children?

o **Be aware – coaches may already be sending you correspondence – know the rules as to what communication is allowed**

This is harder to understand that it looks. Coaches are allowed certain types of contacts and others are not allowed. They will send material to your high school coach to forward to you. They may have the admissions office send you a brochure without mentioning sports. There are many ways around the "contact" rules. Make sure you know what is allowed. Again, the official websites will offer the current contact rules.

o **Be realistic when assessing athletic ability**

Here we are again. Parents, I implore you to be honest with yourselves and with your children about the type of school they should be shooting for. If you son is 5'9" and slow, please don't think they are going to a powerhouse basketball school. There is almost always a bigger, stronger, and faster kid out there. Know where they fit and what school will offer them the best future. Seek out your high school and travel coaches to get advice. If you don't trust them, then start looking around the internet for game film for the schools you want to look at. From there, you should be able to begin making the honest assessment.

o **Talk to your coaches about what colleges you are interesting in attending**

Your coaches are very valuable resources, so use them. Get advice on the schools they played at and where they think your son or daughter fits. They will be more blunt than you may want, but sometimes that bluntness is needed. Use their contacts as much as you can. This is why those personal relationships are so important. Coaches will be more than willing to put their name on the line for your son or daughter if that relationship is strong and they know their word will not be tarnished. Please keep this in mind for all of your conversations with the coach. Also, please know that coaches know which parents are verbally supporting the team and which are berating the other players or coaching staff.

o **Evaluate your athletic goals for college**

It is very important to understand what you want get out of playing a college sport. Do you want to put yourself in a position to play professionally? Do you want to be with a program that will allow you to get the best education and allow you to put school before practices? How much time do you want to spend practicing and traveling? There are many different levels of intensity and you need to figure out which is best for you. If you want to be able to see your children play, they need to stay closer to home. If they hope to learn from a veteran coach and then perhaps seek coaching opportunities for themselves, they need to look in that direction. It is also vital to decide if you want to be a part of a big program or if you want to be on the court or field as much as possible. Is sitting or redshirting as a freshman acceptable or do you want to be out there right away?

o **Develop a personal athletic résumé and/or highlight reel – keep it short and sweet**

Coaches at the college level have a limited amount of time to research and recruit players. They also tend to have very short attention spans. You need to grab them quickly and make your abilities known. If you are able to put a 3 minute highlight clip together, send that and a short résumé (discussed later) to the colleges of interest. I will talk about the highlight reel later, but make sure to present your top plays first as they may not watch more than 15 seconds if not impressed. Think of the stereotypical music producer you have seen in movies who makes their mind up in seconds about an act. This is what coaches do as well. Many schools are now using online video that catalogs all of their games. College coaches may request access to this so remember they may see all of your games, not just your highlights.

o **Send a letter and résumé to coaches whose program you are interested in and haven't heard back from yet**

So, you sent a letter of interest to a school and haven't heard back yet. Maybe you filled out that questionnaire and no one has called you. Don't be afraid to make another call or send another email. Things get lost in the shuffle and as long as you are polite, the coaches usually respond. Understand that the head coach does not keep track of the early part of recruitment. This is left up to assistant coaches until the recruitment gets serious.

o **Follow up with phone calls to coaches**

Since you are now able to contact coaches (in most circumstances), follow up with them to make sure they know of your interest. This is a two-way street as they want to know you are serious about joining their program as well. They are likely recruiting multiple players in your son or daughter's skill level and/or position and might be waiting on the first commitment. A quick phone call can make a big difference and may also let you better know the coach.

o **Follow the seasons on your top school choices – be prepared to speak on them**

Want to impress the college coaches? Then be able to talk intelligently about their team and their current or most recent season. This will let them know how serious you are and may make them more serious in return. It is not enough to know the scores, you want to be able to talk about how those scores came to be and maybe where he or she sees your child fitting in. Bigger schools have lots of footage online, smaller local schools should see you in the stands.

o **Plan to visit colleges during school breaks**

Plan to visit schools during breaks in your school year. Most high schools have limits to the number of college visit days they will excuse and colleges may look at attendance records when making their decisions. For this reason, it is important to prioritize your visits. Have your son or daughter only miss school to go to those that they most want to attend. Others can be visited on weekends or over the holidays. The hard part is seeing what the school looks like when it is most active. Know the "official visit" rules and be careful to follow them. It is okay to let coaches know you are coming, but they may not be able to speak to you due to recruiting rules. You can also contact the coach after your visit to offer your impressions and your desire to attend their school.

o **Schedule a meeting with the coach during these visits**

As long as you are within the visitation rules, try to meet with the head coach or at least an assistant. Don't be afraid to contact coaches that have not contacted you. You may not be on their radar at this point, but if there is a good visit, that may change. Bring your highlight reel and résumé.

o **Keep a journal of your initial impressions and afterthoughts from each visit**

I can't overstate the importance of journaling your thoughts immediately after the visit. The more schools you visit, the more confusing some things can become. Your initial feel and view of the school may differ from your thoughts after doing some thinking. Having that written journal to go back to as you will want to compare your views. Don't fall victim to falling in love with the most recent school or to judging all against your first visit. A template is provided later.

o **Ask high school coaches to make a recommendation for a school choice**

Your high school coaches are a great asset in this process. Use them as often as you can. I am grateful to have had many great relationships with families that led me to doing more than could be expected to help students get into the right school. Unfortunately, I have also seen toxic relationships where demanding and overbearing parents have played the school transfer game while chasing the answers they want, rather than the answers they need. Please remember how helpful your coaches can be and use that to your advantage. They know that your child's success will lead to their own success.

o **Attend camps, clinics, and pro try-out days**

Attend as many of these as you can as long as your son or daughter is able to perform at their peak. These do nothing if the performance is not quality. However, getting in front of scouts, coaches, and any evaluator is crucial. You may impress someone with that one move or one play. First impressions are very important because these people rarely change their minds. Remember, to paraphrase the great Joe DiMaggio, "you play hard because there might be somebody in the standstoday who'd never seen you play before, and might not be able to see you again".

o **Make interested coaches aware of which camps you will attend**

If a college coach has expressed an interest, be sure to let them know which camps your son or daughter will be attending. This allows them to see your child again and also shows your interest in their program. This is an easy contact that goes a long way.

o **Narrow down your college choices to a top 10-12 by the end of summer after your junior year**

This is harder than it may seem, especially for Spring sports athletes. You have to start limiting your expectations and possibilities early so that you don't become overwhelmed or burdened by the process. There is a lot of stress involved in this, but there can be a lot of fun too. By limiting your scope, you can start to have more fun with it. Best suggestion here is to select 4-5 ideal schools and then build your fall back options. There should be several local options as well as community and junior colleges on your list.

o **Send your game schedule to interested college coaches**

The coaches may try to find your schedule if your son or daughter is the elite recruit, but most situations don't look like that. Most require you to get the schedules to the coaches well ahead of time so they can prioritize things. If they express interest, be sure to give addresses and email the day of the game if there are changes or weather issues. Keep in mind that if you want to play a college sport, these coaches are likely in the middle of their seasons at the same time your son or daughter is playing. Basketball season is basketball season at all levels. These coaches have a lot of planning to do and having a schedule sent to them certainly helps. Also understand that college coaches have connections at other schools that may help them scout. So even if your college doesn't get to see you, it doesn't mean there isn't someone watching your son or daughter closely.

Chapter 5

Academic Actions to be Taken During Senior Year

Ok, it is starting to get stressful and you are beginning to become concerned about how this is all going to play out. This year will pass more quickly than you think and it is easy to fall behind in the process. You and your child have a lot to do this year and even if the decision has been made, there can be no quit as things can fall apart at the last minute.

In my personal situation, I was fortunate enough to attend the right baseball camp and meet the right coach. This man saw something in me that others hadn't. A positive relationship with the right person got me started. Soon, his coaching connections had me getting calls and letters from schools I thought were beyond my reach. He helped me get a video (old school, I know) out to prospective schools and suddenly I had scholarship and grant offers coming in. I had my mind up to take an offer at one school and was about to do all of the paperwork when this man took a job at a Division I school. Next thing I knew I had my offer from that school. Unfortunately, my surgically repaired arm injury caught up with me and the 4-year scholarship was altered to become contingent on my health, but it was there nonetheless. Suddenly, Division I baseball was taken away from me and I was left with just my backup option. Thankfully, this turned out to be a blessing in disguise, but it didn't feel that way at the time.

o **Meet with your College Counselor to review NCAA, NAIA, and NJCAA Academic Eligibility Requirements and evaluate your academic progress**

If a scholarship or grant money to play college sports are in your future, you are going to see a lot of your guidance counselor during the senior year. Meet 2-3 times during the year to make sure that all requirements are being met and that there have not been any changes in eligibility rules that may affect things. If a course change is required, make sure this is done right away.

o **Explore more College Guides**

This is hard to grasp at times, but there are schools out there that may be late to the table and come out of nowhere as an option. This can be due to their sudden interest or because you find an academic program that fits your son or daughter better than others you have seen. Keep options open.

o **Continue a challenging academic schedule**

Many colleges will pull scholarships or grants if they see courses pop up on schedules that do not challenge students. A weak schedule is a reflection on your kids and even if you think a school is not looking, they are. Especially if it is a local school. Grades should also be kept high, even through senioritis. Again, try to schedule dual enrollment courses with a local Junior or Community College to get things started.

o **Retake SAT and/or ACT and send to your top 10-12 schools**

Each time the test is taken, it will get easier and the scores will improve. Make sure that your results are being sent to your top 10-12 favorite schools. Oftentimes you can request that your scores are sent automatically to specific schools, and they will have the results right away. If your favorites change along the way, be sure the score is reported to new schools as well. There are lots of great books filled with advice on how to take these tests, but the best advice is to simply apply yourself and find some help if you need it. It may also help to know the minimum score needed for each school.

o **Take AP exams when applicable**

If AP classes are taken, the exam should be taken as well. Every college has different scores that they will accept for credit. If your son or daughter is able to earn college credit while in high school, you need to take advantage of that. The more credits that can be earned when not in-season, the easier it will be to stay on top of academics. The same holds true during college by taking Winter and Summer courses when possible and then taking fewer credits during the season.

- Calculate your GPA and class rank and identify ways to improve them

This is still true even though it is harder to do during your last year of high school. There are ways to take extra classes or independent studies that may help. Even going after extra credit with the teachers to move that B to an A can help. Again, colleges are moving away from these qualifiers, but not entirely. The ranking and GPA will influence their decisions.

- **Choose teachers to write letters of recommendation – must be completed in early September for Early Decision Applications.**

All of those positive relationships you built are now going to start paying big dividends. Ask the teachers that you know will do a good job. You can ask older students who wrote letters for them and who they suggest you ask. These letters should contain a list of clubs, activities, volunteer work, and all things that make your son or daughter special and stand out. The letters should be succinct, but contain enough information to show the relationship between student and teacher. The student should also explain why they want a particular teacher to write a letter for them. As a teacher, if the parent asks for the student or if the student is less than interested in how this works, I am likely not going to write the letter. When students ask and are enthusiastic about it, I will spend a great deal of time writing the best letter I can. Be mindful as these letters can make a difference. They serve as an indicator for the type of student-athlete you have and coaches need as much information as they can get.

- **Continue to participate in clubs and activities and review your college academic goals and interests**

If the situation at your school of choice changes, continuation of activity in your high school will look good. Your son or daughter's goals and interests should continue to be pursued as we have to remember that very few will get paid after college to play a sport. In the end, these goals and interests are the reason for going to college in the first place and sports just provide the vehicle for a free or cheaper education.

- **Make a list of colleges you are interested in attending and get applications**

Many colleges have a common application that is used by many others which certainly eliminates some strain, but some still want you to request a formal application. Find each school's application process and get this process started. The fee for each application may alter your list or force you to narrow them down a bit. Use your filing system and keep things in a neat and orderly fashion for easy access when you need them.

o **Solicit input from as many people that you trust as possible**

Time to ramp up this part of the process. You need to find alumni, coaches, anyone that you can, and ask them about the school, its environment, the coaching staff, and anything else that you value. Keep that journal and start to eliminate schools!

o **Categorize your college list: Reaches-Probables-Safeties: Be sure to apply to at least one of each**

We all grow up dreaming of playing for those popular Division I teams and all that comes with that. Those are probably your "reach" schools. If those are in your ability level, divide those up accordingly as well. These rankings can be based on any of the things that you and your children care about most. The coaches, exposure to professional teams, majors offered, prior financial discussions with the school, close to home, the school you graduated from, even down to quality of the school food if that is what you care about. But getting these schools ranked early will help you later on.

o **Talk with your children about financial needs and YOUR expected contribution**

Again, this is a hard discussion, but if a $40,000 per year school can offer you a ½ scholarship, that still may be out of your price point. This would leave your son or daughter on the hook for a lot of money after graduation. Remember, if you co-sign the loan, which you likely will have to do, you are also on the hook for that money. This may alter your prior list or it may solidify it. It is just important to have honest discussions so you know which schools to make the hard press with and which you can stop wasting time on. This may also be the time to let your children know how much you have already saved up for their college and that you may be willing to give them whatever is left after paying for school. This too may change their minds.

o **Create a scholarship and financial aid application due date timetable**

Your journaling and keeping up to date on your folders will be put to the test. Make sure you are earlier than the due dates so that you can perhaps beat others to the punch. However, you certainly do not want to lose out on an opportunity because you missed a deadline.

o **Apply for grants, loans, financial aid, and scholarships: DO NOT MISS DEADLINES**

This is another part of the journaling and folder keeping that is essential. There are so many scholarships and grants out there that you may feel overwhelmed or worry that they are out of reach. Maintain that folder as best as you can so that you have all of the necessary information at hand at all times. A missed deadline may cost you thousands of dollars. Check with guidance counselors again to make sure that you don't miss any. Most schools have local scholarship award opportunities that can help reduce costs. Every little bit helps.

o **Submit recommendations, transcript and test scores that are requested to your guidance office as early as possible**

Make sure that all needed scores and test results are available to your guidance counselor and on the transcripts as soon as possible. If a school is recruiting your son or daughter, they may contact the guidance office without your knowledge to see if the required scores are reached and if all academics are in order. It is important to fill out the SAT and ACT forms correctly to get your scores to your school as soon as possible.

o **Fill out all College applications and aid requests <u>completely</u> and <u>before deadline</u>**

The earlier, the better. If you can beat others to the submission process, then that is to your advantage. If a coach is deciding between players, often times their mind can be made up for them if one of those players didn't have their paperwork in on time. This sounds like a simple thing, but I have heard several college coaches complain about this problem. If your school of choice is still financially out of reach with the partial sports scholarship your son or daughter earned, having the aid packages completed early may help get your son or daughter into the program of their dreams anyway. Again, it doesn't matter what the money is called, as long as it is there.

o **Be sure to have your essay edited by a trusted teacher – <u>absolutely no mistakes!</u>**

The easiest way to get a scholarship rejected or to have the school flat out not accept your son or daughter's application is to have silly mistakes on it. The application essay is a very important component of the whole process. Please make sure that a trusted teacher proofs and edits the work your son or daughter produces. This is their big shot at impressing an admissions office. You must take advantage of this opportunity. There are hundreds of ways to screw up this application process and only one way to execute things perfectly. That execution is vital.

Chapter 6

Athletic Actions to be Taken During Senior Year

Depending on the sport played, this portion may be different for each athlete. Those playing Fall or even Winter sports are still trying to get noticed by more schools or at least trying to decide between the few that remain interested. Those playing Spring sports are about out of time and need to work extra hard to get noticed by that one coach who can make that life-altering decision. Fall/Winter athletes are likely going to have time after their season to go on visits or to play the slow game with coaches to get as much scholarship or grant money as they can. This is not going to be an option for Spring athletes.

o **Register with the NCAA Clearinghouse if you have not already done so**

You simply cannot play an NCAA sport without this process. The sooner this is off your list the better. This can take longer than expected and you may end up waiting on small items at times. Gathering all of the necessary information may require some gentle reminders to your counselors, so take that person's abilities and even their time into consideration. Make sure to check the Clearinghouse site (https://web3.ncaa.org/ecwr3/) often for updates or changes.

o **Send for a new copy of *NCAA Guide for the College-Bound Student Athlete***

As stated before, this document undergoes changes every year so it is important to locate any changes that affect you. They may alter things in your favor or offer some helpful last minute tips. Please don't lose a scholarship or grant opportunity over a few dollars or because you didn't get this from the guidance office.

o **Know the NCAA rules and regulations surrounding athletic recruitment**

Each level has different rules and regulations about the timing of contacts and number of official visits. Know these as you don't want to have eligibility issues before even arriving at college. Each level also has different calendars about when this contact can begin. Some begin the day after the junior year of school ends, others begin on the first day of class of the senior year or even when those Fall sports start practice. There are even limits to the number of texts and calls that can be made. Be careful to also know when the visits are deemed "official".

o **Provide interested coaches with your game schedule as early as possible**

Any coach or school that contacts your son or daughter should be given a game schedule as soon as it is available. Most game schedules are available several months in advance and your Athletic Director can give you these well ahead of their publication. Get these to your coaches along with the addresses of fields or gyms. It is imperative to contact any coach that is planning to attend a game if there is a change due to weather or any other reason. You can also link schedules to a high school website if it is updated daily. Most coaches will double check before heading to a game. Imagine how the coach would feel about driving a long way to an empty gym or field. I don't believe that would go over very well.

o **Review your college athletic goals with your coaches and be realistic about your ability level**

This is time to get serious about your choices and desires. Time to give up any unrealistic expectations you have about playing ability and any unrealistic college expectations. A student-athlete needs to be at the best school for their own personal and academic needs, not the one they think their parents want them to attend or the one that impresses peers. They need to find the right coach, the amount of playing time desired, the right major, and so many other things that should go into the decision. Make sure to keep those folders updated and hang on to all of your materials. You never know when a coach from an eliminated school may contact you and you have to re-examine what they have to offer.

I have seen too many kids go to the wrong schools for what were they thought were right reasons at the time. They didn't do enough due diligence and paid a hefty price for it. They thought they knew what they wanted based on faulty information or trying to please others. Don't let your children make this mistake. Make sure that they are honest with themselves and that you are honest with them in return. There is a lot of trust that goes into this. The sheer amount of information will feel like a wave crashing down, but if you keep organized and honest with yourselves, you will get through it. Being realistic with ability level is at the core of this decision. Don't let issues that should be on the periphery impact it. I have seen several kids from our small-town area go to city schools only to quit and come home. This delays athletics for sure, but it also delays graduation and costs much more in the long run.

o **Study your top college choices' current roster and your potential playing time**

Again, some players really want to have that Division I jacket or have that big claim later, but will ultimately end up sitting on the bench and perhaps unhappy. Make sure that you are all realistic about expected playing time and what you will be happy with. Be blunt with the coaches and they will be blunt with you. Make sure to also talk to players already in the program to get a feel for what actually occurs rather than just relying on the coach to be fully honest.

o **Add to your achievement file / highlight reel**

Anything that may make your son or daughter more attractive to a school should be sent in when ready. You don't want to bother coaches, but if you wait for them to act, you will be waiting a long time. Again, if you have the straight to the pros kid, this guide is not for you. This is for the player that wants to play a sport in college and use it as a tool to get their education. You must be the door-to-door salesperson.

o **Keep in contact with the coaches who have shown an interest**

Don't let them forget about you! Coaches are inundated with information about prospective players. If they have shown the interest, they want to be informed. You can even ask them upfront when you should contact them again or how often they want to hear from you. Some coaches are a bit scattered during their seasons and will welcome your email or call. Others are on top of things daily and don't want to be disturbed or pestered. Make sure you know who is who.

o **Ask those coaches about official visits and have them help you plan for this event**

This is a great way to find out which coaches are truly interested and which are just fishing. If you ask the coach for dates they want you to have the official visit and they don't communicate with you, they likely don't want to be bothered. However, if they or an assistant actively help set the date and everything that goes with the visit, then you have the start of something. These signals will be loud and clear when you see them. For now, this part may seem a bit obscure, but you will absolutely notice these situations as they arise. You will see a checklist on these visits at the end.

o **Speak openly with college coaches about scholarships and financial aid opportunities – they will help with the aid process**

Coaches have a lot of influence in the admissions office and in the financial aid office. If they want a player on their team, they can do a lot for you. Think of it as a car deal. The coach is the salesperson and he only has so much money to go around. If he can get you to foot the bill and still get his/her athlete, that is what they will do. Just as the salesperson would love for you to pay sticker price. Push them by being honest with your ability to pay. Remember that a financial grant is the same thing as a scholarship. Don't look at it any other way. If they want your son or daughter, they will find the money. Also, if you are uncomfortable talking about the money in front of your child, ask to excuse them. The coaches have seen this before and will not mind.

o **Speak openly with college coaches about your athletic goals and possible playing time and progression during your career**

It is hard to talk about playing time before even getting into a school, but this needs to occur. As stated earlier, coaches like to balance their teams with senior/sophomore and junior/freshman at each position or event. Know if they have a no-freshman start policy or if they play the best player and that is that. Some coaches may stretch the truth here so make sure to talk to current players about this. Also, keep in mind that no coach will guarantee playing time. I have never done this at the high school level, they certainly don't at the collegiate level. They are paid for success, not for keeping everyone happy.

o **Ask a lot of questions**

There are no bad questions when talking to a coach. They understand that they must sell you and your son or daughter and will answer any question they can. Remember, they may not have all of the answers, but hopefully they know where to find them and will get that answer for you later. Be sure that you understand the answers as well. Don't be afraid to clarify a response.

o **Write in your journal after each contact with a school or coach**

Journaling right after a call, email, or visit is necessary to keep all of your facts straight as your initial views and feelings are usually best. Be descriptive about the answers and things that are easy to note, but also take the time to describe the tone and overall feel you have from that contact. The warm and fuzzy stuff can make a difference regarding with whom you trust your children.

o **Continue to follow each top college choice**

Make sure to follow up. A "thank you" card or email to a coach after a visit or even a post on social media may make a difference and keep your son or daughter's name in the coach's head. Follow up with answers to any questions they have for you as well.

o **After You Choose Your College, Finish your senior year strong academically and athletically – do not give them a reason to pull your scholarship or aid**

Make sure that you don't give anyone a reason to doubt your son or daughter's authenticity. They need to finish their high school career on a high note and prevent a college or a coach from regretting their decisions and possibly altering them. This does happen, and it can happen in your favor too. Remember, if you are getting into a school late in the process, that means someone is on their way out. Don't be the person that loses out on a great opportunity.

o **Work to improve your athletic level over the summer – do not go into a season out of shape**

The temptation will be to hang out with friends and take it easy. Those things are all great, but your son or daughter needs to arrive at school in August and be in exceptional physical shape. They want to make a serious impression on the coaching staff for sure, but it is also good to make a positive impression on the upperclassmen.

Chapter 7

Key Areas of Consideration

Below is a list of essential questions to consider when looking at potential schools in the areas of both athletics and academics. It is important to keep in mind that the goal is to use your son's or daughter's athletic gifts to get into a distinguished school and for them to receive the best education possible. All while hopefully having a lot of fun and success in their sport. So you can add these questions to your journals and keep coming back to them. Compare and contrast schools based on how much you value each answer. Maybe even create your own rating system or go with the standard pro/con list. However you do it, just be sure to keep good notes and to keep everything in perspective.

There is a lot to consider in the questions below. Each person will have their own values for each answer and there may be some disagreements with your son or daughter about what is most important in the short and long run. Be ready to step in and eliminate or add schools to the list based on your experience. Sometimes kids get lost in this process and forget the ultimate goals. Keep them on track with your detailed journals and calming influence. When there are two or more schools recruiting your children and their ability, it can get distracting and make them press in the classroom and in competition. Be their steady hand. You may want to start bragging, but try not to do this as your son or daughter may end up on the receiving end of some nonsense. Just try to go about this as a job that needs to be completed and be their guide.

Make sure that you lead them in the direction that is best for them, not you. Sometimes, parents try to fit the round peg in the square hole for the wrong reasons or because they don't have a good enough understanding of the process. Make sure that your son or daughter has their head in reality as well.

1. Academic Interest

- Does this college have your area(s) of interest?
- Is this program respected?
- What are the requirements to get into this program?
- What is the average class size?
- How large are lecture and discussion classes?
- What percentage of students graduate with this major?
- Are tutors available?
- Is there a Job Placement Office?
- What is the graduation rate for the college? Program?
- What percentage of students graduate the program in 4 years?
- What does the campus housing situation look? Where do freshmen live?
- What are the rules about having a car on campus?
- Will you room with other athletes or random selections?
- How many share a room or suite?

2. Athletic Interest

- Do you like the coach? How long has the coach been at the school?
- Is the coach staying for all 4 years?
- What is the direction of the program?
- Do your playing goals match the coach's goals for the team?
- How many games are played and can you handle that schedule in the classroom?
- What are the playing and training facilities like?
- How do you fit into the program? Big fish or little fish?
- How many current and recruited players play your position?
- Does the off-season training fit your expectations and schedule?
- Are you required to be on campus over the summer?
- What are the in and out-of-season requirements?
- How many scholarships are available?
- Is the program fully funded? Do you have to cover any costs?
- Do athletes get priority scheduling?
- Is team housing available?

3. Demographic and Geographic

o What is the size of the community? Does this fit you?
o What is the geographic location and does this fit your desires?
o How close to home or relatives is the school?
o How much would travel to and from school cost?
o How many times would you be able to come home during the year?
o How easily will family be able to visit and cheer you on?
o Is the area similar to where you grew up and can you handle the similarity or difference?

4. Finances

o Can you afford this college?
o What types of financial aid are available?
o Can you afford to pay it back?
o What is the deadline for applying for aid?
o If you do not have a scholarship, can you earn one after your freshman year?
o Is there any help to pay for books and materials? Meals? Training? Housing?
o Can you get an on-campus job for spending money?

5. School Size and Division

o How many total undergraduate and graduate students are enrolled?
o What percent of the student body lives on campus? Commutes?
o What are the living arrangements for freshmen and upperclassmen?
o Are you assured housing?
o What is the social life situation at the school? Activities?
o What is the competitive level? All are different and afford different levels of playing time and other opportunities.
o Would you be happy just being on the team or do you need to play?

Chapter 8

Contacting the Coach

When contacting a college coach, there are a lot of do's and don'ts. This can be an intimidating process, so be aware that what you are saying and doing may be perceived differently than you intend. Choose your words wisely. Below is a guide of how to write letters to coaches. Yes, letters. Emails are impersonal and show a lack of respect for the individual school. Make sure to personalize every item in some way. But, make sure that you don't make silly mistakes and cut and paste the wrong school to the wrong coach. Sadly, I have seen this done a few times. The more personal and descriptive your contacts are, the more relatable your son or daughter will be to the coach. Use what you see below as a template or just copy it almost word for word. Whatever you do, resist being too verbose or the temptation to overly sell your son or daughter's ability. Do not make them out to be the next Mike Trout or Aaron Rodgers.

What to Include in Your Letter to the Coach:

Suggested Items:

- PSAT, SAT, ACT, AP scores
- High School transcript, with GPA and class rank
- Athletic stats and description of abilities (be positive and maybe add a negative or two that you are working hard to correct)
- Your realistic future goals and aspirations
- Current teams and coaches – include contact information
- Date of Birth, current height and weight (don't fudge these)
- Interest in scholarship – state that this is a priority!
- Request a team media guide
- Request an application
- Request a college catalog

Additional things to mention:

o   If a parent or relative is an alumnus
o   Any reference you have from a common friend or former player
o   Other sports you are competing in and awards won
o   Why you are interested in their school/program

Attachments:

o   Copy of test scores and transcripts
o   Personal résumé with highlight reel if possible or link to online video
o   Recommendation letters
o   Your complete schedule and contact information

Sample Letter to the Coach

Date
College Name
Coach's Name
School Address

Dear Coach,

I am interested in receiving information on your baseball program and on the University/College. I plan to pursue a career in early childhood education and strongly believe that your university/college is a strong option for me.

For the past three years, I have played shortstop and pitcher for the varsity baseball team at Union High School. I earned All-League honors last year and am working hard to repeat this honor this year. I have also attended several summer camps and played in a competitive fall league for several years. During the off-season, I played for the Baseball Stars Travel program and also was a starter on my high school football and basketball teams.

Please find enclosed my personal résumé providing information on my academic and athletic accomplishments. I have also included copies of my transcript, SAT scores, and recommendations from my teachers and coaches. My varsity schedule is also included and I notice that your team will be in my area on May 2nd. I have also included a short highlight reel that only begins to scratch the surface of what I feel I can offer your fine program.

My Uncle, Robert Smith, graduated from your college in 2008 and earned a teaching certification. He has recommended your college as a perfect fit for me.

Please send me information about your program and an application if possible. I am interested in visiting your program during your Fall season. Please be aware that I will need financial assistance in order to attend college.

Thank you for your time and consideration. I look forward to receiving information from you on the college and the baseball program.

Sincerely, Joe Smith
Address, Phone, Email

Sample Personal Résumé

Name
Address
City, State, Zip
Phone
Email

Birthdate:	**Height:**
Social Security Number:	**Weight:**
Graduation Date:	**Best time to call:**
GPA:	
Class Rank:	
SAT:	
PSAT:	
ACT:	

Scholastic Accomplishments:

National Honor Society – 11,12	High Honor Roll – 9,10,11,12
Student Council – 10,11	School Newspaper – 11,12
Peer Tutor – 9,10,11,12	

High School Baseball
- High School:　　　　　School name
　　　　　　　　　　　　School street
　　　　　　　　　　　　School city, state, zip
　　　　　　　　　　　　Athletic office phone

- Coach:　　　　　　　　Coach's name and contact information

- Awards:　　　　　　　List all awards, team record, main statistics, and anything that helps your cause without bragging.

Summer/ Fall Baseball:
List team and coaches and any special statistics and accomplishments of note

Chapter 9

Campus Visits

The campus visit can be one of the most enjoyable experiences of this entire process. You will get to spend some quality time with your son or daughter while getting the full-court press by the college and the coach as they try to sell you on their program. There are a lot of positives that come from these visits as you can get a real feel for the school and the campus, while also gaining a direct view of the athletic program and facilities. Try to plan these with some time in between as you don't want the visits to run together which may lead to some confusion. Give yourselves enough time to make a quality journal entry and to reflect on how each particular school and athletic program make you feel. However, sometimes you just know the right one when you see it. If that happens, after counting your blessings, put the pressure on the coach and get that money flowing.

Planning a visit:

Plan your visit well in advance and allow yourself at least one full day to visit each college. Some programs want you to have an overnight visit. If that is the case, make sure that your son or daughter grasps the weight of such a night. They must be on their best behavior. Be sure to take notes of each visit and understand that during the summer, the campus may have a different atmosphere than during the regular academic year when all the students are on campus. Also, weekend and holiday visits may be different than a visit during the school week. Don't get thrown by weather and seasonal issues that may enhance or lower a school in your eyes. See things for what they are.

Finally, it is crucial to remember that as much as you are trying to sell yourself to the school and program, they have to sell themselves to you as well. Make sure that all of your questions are answered as you don't want to leave unsure of key items.

Things to be sure to do:

- Schedule appointments with:
- Admissions
  - Interview (if available)
  - Campus tour
- Coach
- Financial Aid Office
- Department of major interest

- Know the college
- Academic requirements; average GPA, Class Rank, SAT or ACT
- Majors offered
- Size and demographics
- Coach's name and how long they have been with the program
- NCAA Division, Conference, and number of scholarships available
- NAIA affiliation or NJCAA conference if applicable
- Team Win/Loss record and finish in league play and overall during the prior year or current record if in-season
- Education mission (Liberal Arts or Pre-Professional)

- Make a list of questions
- Admissions office
- Coaches
- Financial Aid Office
- Students

- Book travel plans early
- Airline reservations
- Hotel reservations
- Car rental
- Overnight dorm stay

On the Campus Visit:

Again, plan your visit well in advance and give yourself a good full day to see each college. You will soon get the idea that you and you son or daughter need to ask a lot of questions. You are going to get a lot of them as well so be ready.

Things to be sure to do on your visit:

o   Meet with admissions – ask questions
o   Meet with the coach – ask questions
o   Meet with financial aid – ask questions
o   Take a tour of the campus
o   Library
o   Labs and studios
o   Computer centers
o   Special facilities
o   Recreational facilities
o   Talk to students – ask questions
o   Attend a class if possible
o   Tour the dorms and dining facilities
o   Visit the career placement center
o   Walk around without a guide to get a better feel
o   Visit the student union, auditorium, sports facilities, concert/play hall, or other areas you may be interested in
o   Eat at a local hangout for students - not the fast food places, but those that are favored by the students
o   Send a follow-up letter to everyone you meet, especially if you are still interested in the college
o   Make notes immediately after your visit
o   Remember to make eye contact – this is very important when interviewing with coaches and admissions
o   Make a good physical impression with your dress and grooming
o   Speak in a clear and strong tone

Questions You May Be Asked By An Admissions Representative

Remember to bring all of your transcripts, test scores, and school profile along with you to the interview. Arrive early to your appointment. Being on-time is like being late at a college. Even if they make you wait it is okay as you never want to make them wait. Present yourself well by dressing and grooming properly. You need to ask as many questions as they do to ensure that this school is a good fit for you. Don't leave with unanswered questions as they will affect your final decision. Promptly send a thank you note after the interview.

Possible Questions From An Admissions Representative:

o   Why are you interested in going to college?
o   What does a college education mean to you?
o   If you did not attend college, what would you do?
o   What courses interested you in high school?
o   What courses interest you in college?
o   Tell us about your high school – best and worst features.
o   What was the most difficult class you had in high school?
o   Why do you believe you will be successful at this college?
o   What social media sites are you active on and what are your screen names?
o   What are you academic goals?
o   Describe yourself. Include strengths and weaknesses.
o   Describe your extracurricular activities
o   Who has been the most inspirational person in your life and why?
o   Name a book that you read recently.
o   What book has affected your thought process?
o   What type of books do you like to read?
o   Do you have a favorite author?
o   If you were to pick a teacher of the year at your school, who would you choose and why?
o   Where do you see yourself in 10 years?
o   What are your thoughts on _____ current event?
o   Tell us about a recent event that affected your life?

Questions You Should Ask of An Admissions Representative:

o   Why are students choosing this college?
o   What are the top reasons I should attend this college?
o   What do you think students like best about this college?
o   Are the Professors available to assist students and what are the usual times? *as an athlete, these times are important due to missed class time*
o   Who teaches the lectures? Labs?
o   Are all courses taught in person or are some online?
o   What does this college offer that other schools don't?
o   Are there any upcoming changes to courses or buildings?

o   What has been the most controversial issue the school has faced in the last 5 years? What happened?
o   What is the most popular major?
o   What are the typical course requirements?
o   What is the graduation rate?
o   Athletes' graduation rate?
o   What are some of traditions at the school?
o   What are the school crime rates?
o   Are there college police officers?

The Financial Aid Office:

o   What scholarships are available to incoming freshmen?
o   Where do I get the scholarship applications?
o   What additional financial aid is available to students other than the Free Application for Federal Student Aid (FAFSA)?
o   What areas of study are grants available for?
o   Where can I find a list of available financial assistance?
o   What scholarships are available after freshman year?
o   How often do I need to renew my application(s)?
o   Do you have any additional suggestions on where to find assistance?
o   Can you give me an estimate on how much financial assistance I might qualify for?

Coaches:

o   What is your coaching philosophy?
o   What are your goals for the program?
o   What would be your goals for me?
o   Can you describe a typical in-season practice? Off-season?
o   What are you academic expectations for your players?
o   How many hours per week are required for weight training? Who runs that program?
o   Is there a dietary program and who runs it?
o   Are study halls offered? What academic support is offered for athletes?
o   Are there opportunities for summer sports near campus? Help with placement?
o   What happens to my scholarship if I suffer a season-ending injury? Career ending?

- o Can scholarships be taken away mid-year?
- o Am I able to get a part-time job to cover expenses?
- o What are the team rules and policies? How are they enforced?

Students:

- o Why did they choose this college?
- o What do you like most about this college?
- o What do you like the least?
- o How easy is it to register for classes that you want and need?
- o What has been your largest and smallest class?
- o How accessible are professors? Do they have time to assist you?
- o Do professors encourage study groups?
- o Who teaches your classes - the professor or a graduate assistant?
- o Do students often skip classes?
- o What has been your favorite class and why?
- o What was the most difficult adjustment you had to make from high school to college?
- o How did you handle it?
- o Did you consider any other school?
- o What do you miss about home?
- o How many hours a week do you study?
- o Where do you study?
- o Are the dorms quiet?
- o Have you ever used a tutor? Result?
- o What are the food options? How expensive is off-campus food?
- o How do you get between classes?
- o Can freshmen have a car on campus? If not, where is it kept?

Current Player:

- o How does the team look this year?
- o How does everyone get along?
- o Is there any hazing?
- o What is the training like?
- o Is the coach approachable? Does he/she keep you informed?
- o What are his/her strengths and weaknesses?

- What is the team good at doing?
- What is an area of struggle?
- What does my position look like? Team depth?
- Is the team united?
- What do you do for fun?
- Who do you hang out with the most?
- What has surprised you the most since you got here?
- What has disappointed you?

Visit Notes

It is best to record notes on your impressions and thoughts immediately after a college visit while everything is fresh in your mind. When you visit multiple schools on one trip, it is recommended that notes be written on each campus prior to visiting the next one. Below is a list of what you should note after each trip.

- College name, location and date of visit
- Contact person and their contact details (Remember to send a thank-you note)
- Your first impression of the college
- Your academic evaluation
- Your athletic evaluation
- Your financial options at the college
- What is student life like?
- The college size / demographics / facilities
- Least impressive feature of the college
- Most impressive feature of the college
- Overall comments
- Can YOU be happy at this college? If so, why?

Chapter 10

Admission Process

The Application

Transcript:

o How challenging are the courses you took in high school? Did you take honors?
o How many credits did you earn?
o How did you do? Grades? Rank?
o Does the course selection match your interests of study?

Test Scores:

o PSAT
o SAT
o ACT
o Achievements such as National Honor Society
o AP Exams and scores

Extracurricular Activities:

o Variety and time spent in clubs and activities. Do a few well, rather than many just to list them
o Experience in an area of interest
o Travel
o Volunteer work – especially with your local athletic association
o Leadership opportunities
o Jobs – summer and after-school

Essay:

o   BE YOURSELF – write from your heart, not what you think others want to hear
o   Be original – do not just get something from the internet, even if you adapt it
o   Correct grammar and spelling are critical
o   Have a teacher proofread to ensure that you have not made any mistakes
o   Do not over edit and lose your content or character
o   Keep within the given guidelines for length and number of words
o   Read the whole application before starting to fill it out
o   Give yourself plenty of time to think and write
o   Ask for help, but make sure that it is your work

The essay should say, "This is who I am and this is how I deal with life." Keep in mind that good college essays are often written as a story or as a conversation.

Recommendations:

o   Develop good student/teacher, athlete/coach, and student/counselor relationships
o   Best choices for letters: Head Coach, Counselor, Someone you worked for or volunteered with, Your favorite teacher who you trust and who knows you well
o   Give them plenty of notice, at least a month before the letter is due, and make sure they will write a positive note

The Interview:

o   Make an appointment
o   Relax, this is also a time for you to interview them to make sure you want to attend their college
o   Ask all of your questions – Don't regret not asking anything you think is important
o   Be yourself and try to get comfortable
o   Make a good first impression with your dress, grooming, and language
o   Maintain eye contact and try to not fidget or show your nervousness

About the National Collegiate Athletic Association (NCAA)

The NCAA consists of over 1,100 U.S. colleges and universities, and it functions as a non-profit organization that is responsible for regulating the athletic programs and athletes in the participating schools. The NCAA is divided into Division I, Division II, and Division III levels of play. Divisions I and II are able to offer athletic scholarships, while Division III will still recruit athletes but will instead use grants to recruit athletes. Same thing and result, just a different name.

NCAA Division I football has further complicated things when it was divided in 2006 into Division I-FBS (Football Bowl Subdivision), Division I-FCS (Football Championship Subdivision), and Division I-Non Football. All other sports use the I, II, and III delineations only. Each level has its own unique eligibility requirements that are adjusted often. They can be found on their official website (http://www.ncaa.org/student-athletes/future). For those that are looking to attend the bigger schools with the most fervent supporters, make sure that you understand the benefits rules that define eligibility and that you have planned for their strict guidelines for high school coursework. There is no easy fix if your planning didn't monitor these courses and adhere to the guidelines.

About the National Allegiance of Interscholastic Athletics (NAIA)

Where the NCAA stays within the United States, the NAIA has included schools from Canada and even the Virgin Islands. Most schools are still found in the United States.

The NAIA focuses on what they call a "Return on Athletics" where they promote schools that offer a better coordination between the athlete and their academics and future beyond sports. They also have some more simple eligibility rules that may become important if you have waited too long to become properly aligned with the NCAA's rules. NAIA schools are also more likely to be private schools.

About the National Junior College Athletic Association (NJCAA)

The NJCAA is an association of junior and community colleges that offers 3 divisions of play that offer varying allowances for financial aid to student-athletes. The Division I schools are able to offer full scholarships which can cover tuition, room & board, and even books. Division II can offer a partial scholarship that can cover tuition and books, but not room & board. NJCAA Division III cannot offer any scholarships for athletics.

Addendum

Pandemic Update

As we navigate through our "new normal", there have been a few adjustments to how college coaches contact prospective athletes and on what the schools are requiring. Here are a few of the key items to keep in mind as we go forward.

1. SAT scores may not be needed, but you still should take them. I have had contact with a bunch of college coaches over the past few years and they continue to talk about their schools devaluing the SAT score. Not that the score is irrelevant, but schools are aware of how many scores do not reflect the ability of the students.

Schools are focusing more on the whole student rather than a simple test. They have always wanted well-rounded students, but now have placed a lot more emphasis on the entirety of the student. This means they are looking at all activities and academic growth. They understand that many students struggled mightily with the pandemic and have learning gaps that have affected their ability to score well on standardized tests. Therefore, they want to see kids that have shown resilience and tenacity by starting to overcome these challenges.

If your son or daughter has had a few rougher years, it is not the end of their journey. Please make sure they use this for their college essay in their application and make coaches aware of this as well. Some of the conversations I have had with coaches have centered on this point. They can navigate through lower SAT scores if they really want your child to attend their school, but they need help to show the admissions office why the chance should be given.

As far as classroom scores go, coaches have a real understanding of the challenges that many faced during virtual learning and how many kids may not have the highest grade point average. So they may not worry too much about that number, but will focus on growth. If your son or daughter had lesser grades during the pandemic, but are starting to shine more now, that matters! Make sure to focus on that growth as it shows maturity, resilience, and determination to succeed. All traits they want in a prospective student-athlete.

2. Get your videos together! Coaches have struggled to fill some positions as many of their assistants have moved on and have not been replaced. Some colleges had hiring freezes and have cut other positions. Since there has already been a sharp decline in college attendance, the chances that an athlete wants to stay on as a graduate assistant has also shrunk. Coaches just don't have the help they need to fully evaluate everyone they want to see.

Most schools have online video programs that can be edited to show highlights. Make sure you get on that early and keep updating them. There are also a bunch of online sites that you can pay for to create a video. Make sure that the video doesn't just show fancy plays. It needs to also focus on the fundamentals of your sport as coaches know that every kid has made some special plays. They want to see the basics too.

One mistake many people make with the video is that they fail to highlight their student-athlete properly. Programs that most high schools use have a feature to focus on individuals. You want to use that as much as possible. At the same time, make sure to also show your child as part of the whole. Parents can focus on scores, goals, spikes, or other things that get attention, but coaches know the value of the little things. Sometimes your son or daughter is such a focus of an opponent that another teammate is able to shine. College coaches understand this and appreciate that as much as a flashy play.

3. Coaches are requesting access to social media sites now more than ever. An area coach told me how their school pulled back a scholarship after the college found a "burner" account that was used and had some questionable content. Coaches and/or school administrators are starting to even ask for the passwords for these accounts. They want to make sure that they aren't embarrassed later. The best thing an athlete can do when looking for a scholarship is to keep all social media accounts basic. Post funny pet memes and sports highlights, but that is it.

Also know that some schools have hired social media experts to back check all incoming students and to monitor their current athletes. Another school has even started to check the social media of the parents. Be careful what you post. If you wonder if it might be questionable, don't post it.

4. With the struggles schools had during the pandemic to get through some courses and keep everyone moving forward, there may be course requirement issues. Make sure you have your son or daughter check with their counselors or coaches to verify that they have completed all of the mandatory NCAA or NAIA courses. Schools are not focused on the SAT test as much anymore, but they are steadfast on these requirements.

Many coaches have also begun to push prospective student-athletes toward community colleges to fill credit or score issues. Community colleges have become a recruiting ground for many colleges and universities. Most college coaches have developed strong relationships with community college coaches. The community college can act as a recruiting ground and as a pipeline for particular schools. Check which community college your university of choice favors and do your research to put your son or daughter in the best possible situation.

5. Tournament teams and high school seasons can work together. Most college staff have the ability to attend events all year round. Others are struggling to have staff to send out during their season. Since the sport your son or daughter plays likely runs their high school season the same time as the college season, you may have to pay for a tournament team in the off-season to catch the right eye. But remember, once you are on one coach's radar, you are on many. Coaches talk and share. If they can't find a spot, college coaches will share with peers if they like the "person" enough.

That said, don't wear out your son or daughter. Too much active time in one particular sport can lead to muscle fatigue and cause injury. The tournament teams might be needed to get seen, but they also don't put the effort into body care that high schools do. High schools have trainers and coaches at the ready and monitor mental and physical health. Almost all high schools also have relationships with local hospitals including highly skilled trainers at all practices and events. This protects your child far more than a trainer or two working at tournament events which include hundreds of kids. Additionally, high school programs run daily and coaches see things that tournament coaches just can't as their schedules are vastly different.

6. College visits have also changed with the pandemic. Schools went a few years

without this tool and some have all but abandoned college visits. They want you to come and stay, but no longer want the potential hassle that comes with an overnight stay. Be ready to visit the school with your son or daughter and stay at a local hotel instead. It is safer in many, many ways.

Set these up as early as possible so that you don't have issues with scheduling conflicts. The hardest part of these visits is making sure you don't conflict your visit with your high school schedule. Check with those coaches before finalizing anything with the college. College coaches want responsible kids. This shows that type of behavior.

7. We'll end the update with everyone's favorite topic, vaccines. Yes, vaccines may not be a favorite thing to discuss publicly. But just like all of those vaccines your son or daughter likely received as a child, almost all public colleges and a vast majority of private colleges now require a Covid-19 vaccine before visits and certainly before entering college classrooms. Check with your school counselor on a college's policy and make your decisions from there.

Notes

Acknowledgements

This guide would not have been possible without a lot of help along the way. First, my wonderful parents ran me to every practice and never missed a game. Their efforts during my college search are what got me started with this process, and their support helped me get started in the coaching field. They still show up to games today!

Regarding my coaching and playing experience, a huge thanks goes to Tom Shive. He was the best coach I ever had and impacted my life beyond the game. While I have worked with so many awesome people over the last thirty years, I must thank some of the most inspiring and brilliant coaches with whom I have coached. I apologize to those I miss. Thank you Jeff Jacksits, Mark Seremula, Emily Biechy, Greg Csencsitz, Lee Seras, Carl Brosious, Ron Genicola, Tim Ardos, Carl Cavallo, Matt Greenplate, Christian Bensing, and Mike Schneider. I would also be remiss if I didn't mention the editing help and corroboration from Matt Scholl and Dave Remaley.

Of course, none of this would be possible without Tammy Seidick. She is the most supportive and amazingly talented wife a guy could have. My sons, Mickey and Danny, have also allowed me to spend so much time away while coaching. Finally, thank you to all of the athletes I have been lucky enough to coach. From those players with tremendous talent that led me to gain knowledge to create this handbook to those players that were just plain fun to be around. I have enjoyed watching all of you grow into distinguished and successful adults. Thank you.

About the Author

The information and recommendations in this guide come from coaching a combined 32 seasons of varsity baseball and basketball and working with some extremely impressive athletes. I was also fortunate enough to have gone through the process myself many years ago. At first, I was only able to help student-athletes using my own personal experience, but as the years and athletes added up, I created a small version of this guide that I would give to all of my incoming freshman to use along the way. Now, I am attempting to pass this on to a wider audience with much deeper explanation and description without being too loquacious.

My experiences being recruited as a Division I baseball player were very confusing. We got material from more schools than I could count and I had a stack in my room that was waist high. It was just too much. I didn't realize at the time that most of it was essentially junk mail with few real options include. Thankfully, I met a coach at a camp that was the perfect match for me. He was scout for a pro team at the time and he took an interest in me. I was not MLB draft material, so he wasn't looking at me for that, but saw enough to try and get me to the right school. He passed my name on to a few schools and helped me narrow things down. But I really lucked into things when he took an assistant position at a Division I school about 2 hours away.

That was the good part. The bad part began long before I met this scout. Athletes were not treated as carefully as they are today and all of those little league curve balls caught up to me. I had to have ulnar collateral ligament surgery after my junior year of high school. Throwing was painful, but the doctors promised that I wasn't doing any more damage and the scholarships needed to be earned, so I played. Today, the recovery time would be 10-12 months, but I only spent 6 weeks in a sling and then was back at it soon after. This is when I met that scout. I signed with his school and even went to orientation in August before practice began. However, my elbow acted up and my 4-year offer turned into a year-by-year one that would be contingent on my arm health. I wasn't as enthusiastic about the school as I should have been as it didn't really offer the major I wanted so I quickly reversed course, much to my parents dismay, and enrolled in the nearby state school to become a teacher. Turned out to be the best life decision I've ever made. I tried to keep playing, but the toll was just too much on a daily basis.

From there, I started coaching at my old high school to fill my competitive desire and was hooked on coaching. Since that time, I have played ever expanding roles in helping student-athletes navigate the college scholarship process. Early in my coaching career I was lucky enough to coach a wonderful young man who ended up as a 12th round draft pick of the Los Angeles Dodgers. He had a full college scholarship already, but didn't have the resources to engage any lawyer or agent in the signing process so I stepped into that roll. The key point I made sure was covered during his signing negotiation was that the organization understand the value of the college scholarship he was giving up. I was able to help negotiate triple what was initially offered per year and for a longer time period. The best part was that a contingency was put in the contract where the Dodgers also agreed to pay for his education after his career was finished depending on his career earnings.

I had already been making mental notes at this time, but during this process I began to journal and note all of these interactions. I also began to put my other experiences in writing as a template to give to future star athletes. After designing the initial bare-bones template, I always had to further explain the meanings of the notes. The guide was good, but I often felt that I would miss something in explaining the subtle nuances of the process to each new athlete. A more full guide was written many years ago, but now I have fleshed it out as much as possible while trying to keep it simple and short enough to be an easy thing to follow.

I have been very fortunate to have directly coached many athletes that have earned money for college from their athletics. Obviously, not every one of them became a professional, but they all found a way to use their athletic gifts and efforts to become teachers, physical therapists, nurses, and so much more. This is the real goal. I am always filled with pride and joy when I see a former player who has reached their dreams and know that I played even the smallest role in that.

In this guide, I try to offer many inside tips and suggestions to help you make the perfect decision on which school fits you the best. College coaches always want the best athletes, but they also want the players that will stay at their school and become a valuable member of their program. They want to win, but they also want to work with good kids. Making the right decision the first time will also allow you to finish school more quickly and put you on pace to reach your goals as planned. I am very proud that almost all of the athletes that I coached have remained at their chosen school and completed their degree. I am confident that the information in this guide will help you make the correct choice as well. Above all, please remember that you should choose the school that best fits your future career and academic goals, yet has the athletic program that will make the college experience everything you desire.

Made in the USA
Las Vegas, NV
20 September 2023

77875031R00042